6 Inventive Solos

for Playing and Optional Improv

Parts Included for "Jamming" with Friends

By Bert Konowitz

Edited by Cynthia Pace

Have fun—Reach out to others for a musical "social-media" experience!

These six Jazz, Rock and Pop style pieces provide unique options for performing either with friends, family, teacher, or audience, or individually. Add the varied accompaniments or play as solos. Great for both social and individual settings.

2433

CONTENTS

Text Me Some Jazz

(Call and Response)

Moderate—Steady and even eighths

Bert Konowitz

"Text:" Create the same melody in both hands. Use e♭, e, g or a with these rhythms.
13
16
19
22
mf
mp
mf
mp
f
Hold up your cellphone, pretending to text.

Stomp Your Foot

(Syncopation*)

Blues Jazz March

Bert Konowitz

Clap
Clap
Stomp
Stomp
Jam—Change the dynamics on each repeat
Repeat 3 times
Stomp:
Audience

Whose Blue Note Is It, Anyway?!

(Blue Notes*)

Easy and relaxed, Swing Eighths

Bert Konowitz

13
Stop, wait, then go on
Speak: Blue Notes?
Point to Blue Notes being played and say:
"G_flat's_a___ blue__ note, E__flat's_a___blue__note"
NO!
17
a tempo
p
mf
21
Clap/Tap
Clap/Tap
23
Spoken
It's
Mine!
fz
MINE !
Whose Blue Note is it?
It's
Mine!
MINE!

Knock, Knock, Who's There? Dorian! (Mode)

Bert Konowitz

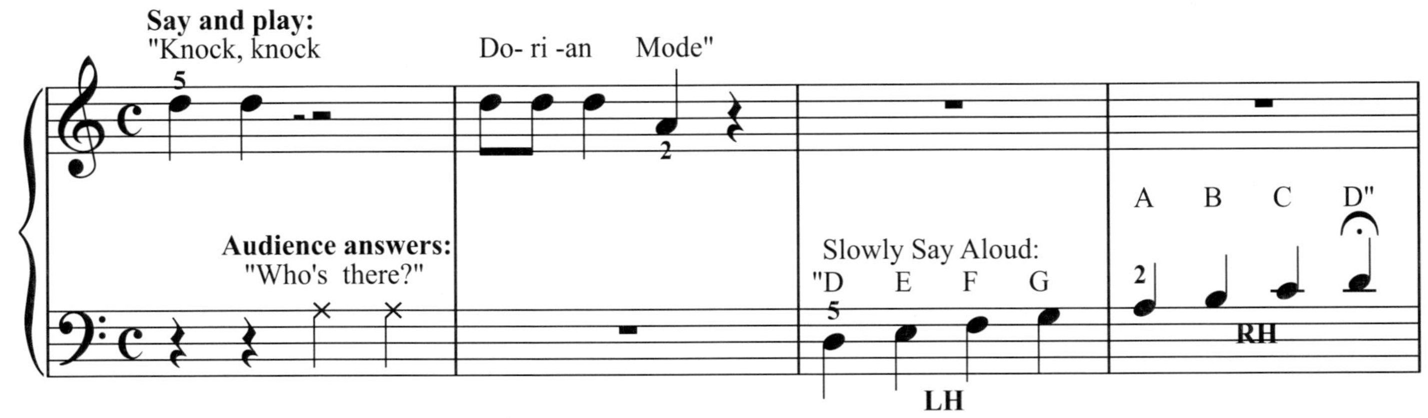

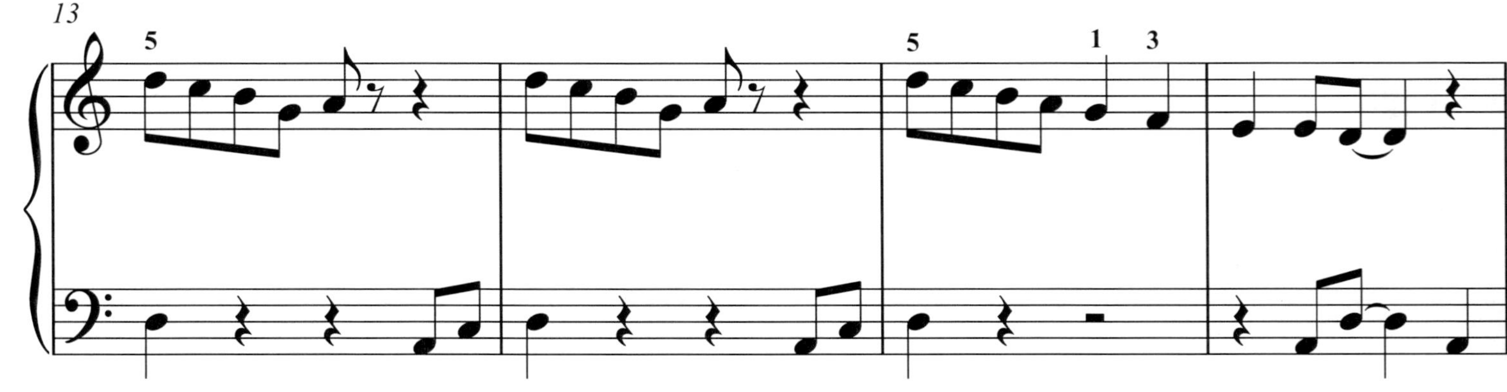

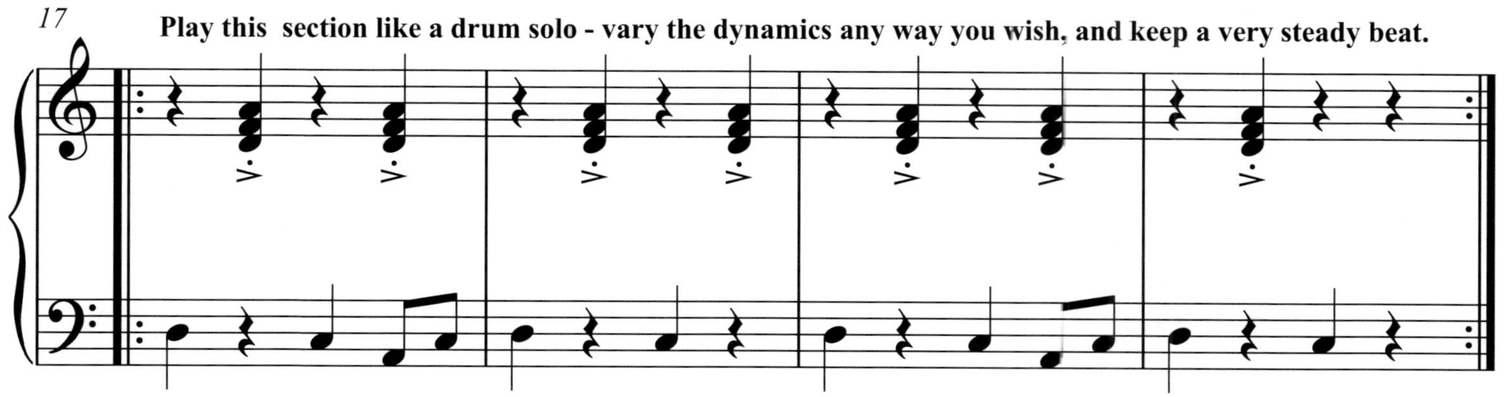
17
Play this section like a drum solo - vary the dynamics any way you wish, and keep a very steady beat.

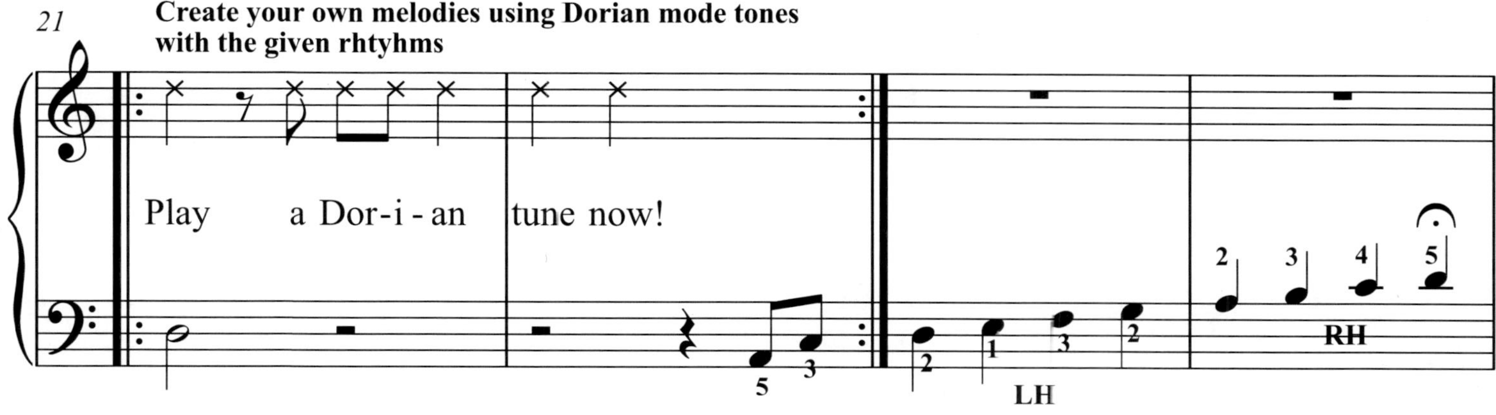
21
Create your own melodies using Dorian mode tones
with the given rhtyhms
Play a Dor-i-an tune now!
LH
RH

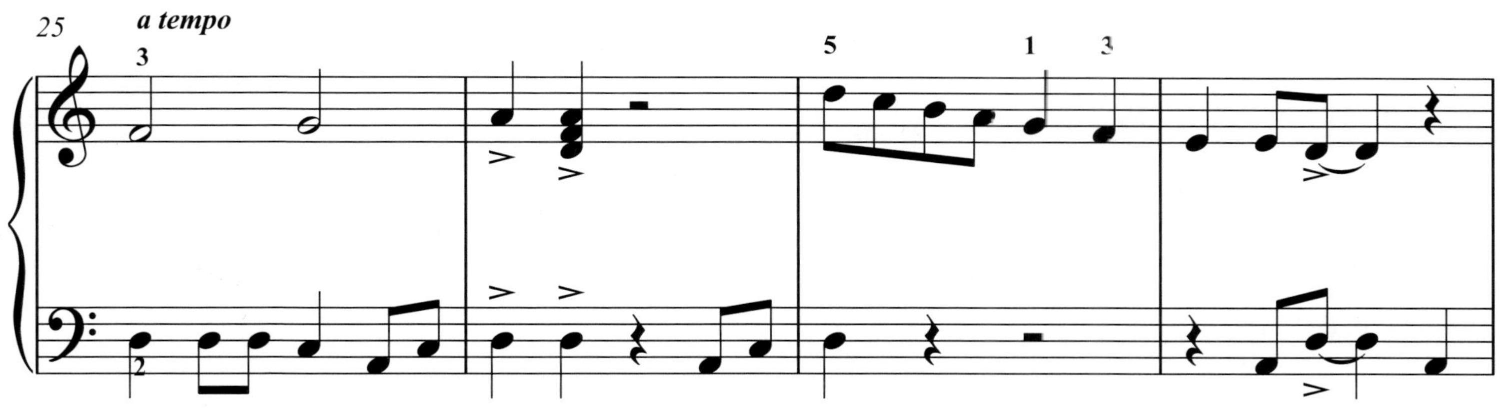
25
a tempo

29
p
Dor-i-an Mode!

Play It Again, Again, and Again

(Riffs *)

Bert Konowitz

12
mp
subito p
14
mp
mf
17
mp
21
Repeat 3 times
Speak:
"Enough?"
"Yes!"
"Yes"

Easy Walkin' Blues

(Walking Bass and Comping*)

Bert Konowitz

*Comping: Short chords used to accompany another player's solo

17
F7
F7
C7
Dr.
21
G7
F7
C7
Dr.
25
mf
Optional: Play LH one octave lower than written, ms. 25 -28.
Dr.
29
f
Dr.